THE KOVELS' BOOK OF ANTIQUE LABELS

Ralph and Terry Kovel

Historic packaging designs for decoration & appreciation

KNICKERBOCKER BISCUIT CO.

SELECT SODA CRACKER

SELECT SODA CRACKER

CRISP, TENDER, NOURISHING DELICIOUS

SODA SELECT

Crown Publishers, Inc.   New York

Inquiries should be addressed to Crown Publishers, Inc., One Park Avenue, New York, New York 10016.

Manufactured in the United States of America
Published simultaneously in Canada by General Publishing Company Limited

Library of Congress Cataloging in Publication Data
Kovel, Ralph M.
    The Kovels' book of antique labels.
    1. Labels. 2. Decoration and ornament.   I. Kovel,
Terry H.   II. Title.   III. Title: Book of antique labels.
NC1002.L3K6   1981   741.6′9   81-15226
                              AACR2

ISBN: 0-517-544970

Design by Joanna Nelson

10 9 8 7 6 5 4 3 2 1

First Edition

INTRODUCTION

A Brief History of Labels

The notion of a label to identify either the contents of a package or the maker of its ingredients goes back to ancient times. Jars from ancient Greece were marked with names; clay seals identified goods sold by the Babylonians. Packaging as we know it began in the sixteenth century, when traders and merchants began wrapping some of their products in paper with the product identified on the outside in writing. Medicines with an identifying label on the outside of the package, wine bottles wrapped in paper bearing the innkeeper's name, and tobacco packed in printed paper wrappers appeared in the 1660s. By the 1700s, pins, drugs, and some groceries, especially teas, were sold in paper packages stamped with labels, while condiments, ointments, and snuff were offered up in bottles or jars with printed labels glued to the outside. In the mid-nineteeth century, with the invention of papermaking machines and the process of lithography, labeling became even more common. The oldest known American label in existence is from a package of paper made at the Luke Bemis Mill in Watertown, Massachusetts, in about 1799.

Packaging in tin cans, a striking innovation, began in the early 1800s. Tins were patented in France in 1810, and by 1813 foodstuffs were being canned for the entire British army. The first tin cans commercially manufactured in America appeared in 1819. Ezra Daggett and Thomas Kensett patented their containers in 1825, and they soon developed a successful business selling fruit, oysters, tomatoes, and other foods in cans. Another innovator, William Underwood, came from London to Boston in 1821 and began selling sauces and pickles, and later tomatoes, deviled ham, and milk—all in cans.

By the time of the Civil War, canning had become an important business, particularly in the United States. Although paper-labeled cans were used, tins with labels painted directly onto the metal became very popular. The earliest known printed can in America was manufactured about 1850 by Reckow and Larne of New York City. It was for tomatoes but, oddly, was painted blue, with an elaborate picture of its red contents engraved on the side. About the same time, lithographed cans came into common use. By 1866, when tooth powder first appeared in a tin, canning had replaced paper-packing for many products.

Paper labels, however, continued to be used on cans as well as on many other types of containers. Crackers, matches, soap, cleaners, needle cases, ink, tea, coffee, cosmetics, sugar, and flour continued to be packaged in cardboard or wooden boxes and usually bore a paper label for identification.

Manufacturers quickly realized that the label served not only as identification but also as a small advertisement for their product. As a result, elaborate printing and eye-catching artwork began to be featured. Shortly after the Civil War, the "attractive woman" became a popular motif, and by the 1880s pictures of company buildings and medals showing awards were commonplace. Cars, trains, balloons, as well as golf and baseball motifs, were introduced as decoration as these ideas became popular with the public. Special trademarks, introduced as early as 1864, when the Bull Durham steer was first used, served the double purpose of both being appealing to look at and supplying instant identification. The Quaker Oats man appeared in 1876, the Baker's Chocolate lady in 1883, the Mennen Talc baby in 1892, and the Cream of Wheat man in 1893. Many of these trademarks became very famous, and in some cases they continue to be used today.

A Word about Collecting Labels

Today, collecting antique labels from foodstuffs and advertising has become one of the most popular interests of collectors. Many restaurants are decorated with old advertisements, "country stores" are fully stocked with old bottles and boxes (and imitations of old bottles and boxes!), and many people have begun using old labels and advertisements to decorate their homes. Moreover, the old labels themselves have become more and more valuable as collectibles.

The various design elements are the keys to establishing the age and value of antique labels. With a little knowledge of the history of printing, one can quickly learn to date a label. The very early labels were often made from woodcuts, then colored by hand. As printing techniques became more sophisticated, designers introduced engraving, stenciling, embossing, lithography, and mezzotint, until finally, today, labels are printed by modern photographic printing methods.

The styles of the artwork and the typography also help to date a label. It seems that most packaging designs reflect styles that were just going out of style, as it were. In other words, when the Art Nouveau style became popular in packaging in the early 1900s, it mirrored a style that had been prominent in the other decorative art fields for more than ten years.

It is almost impossible today to obtain the originals of the labels that appear in this book. Labels are delicate and highly perishable and, thus, many have been lost or destroyed over the years. Also, because collecting labels has become more popular, they seem to have become less and less available—and more and more costly. We bought the Shaker String Beans label that appears in this book almost thirty years ago for just a few dollars; recently, we learned that the identical label is now selling for more than $300!

How to Use This Book

We very much wanted to publish this book for the simple reason that we love antique labels! We have been collecting them for decades, and we have literally thousands of them in drawers and files in our home. We find their beauty stunning, and we are perpetually fascinated by their variety. It has been our experience that both artists and historians respond to the labels the same way we do, and it is our hope that they will find this small collection both useful and pleasurable.

When we decided to publish this part of our collection, we thought it would be fun to print the labels "life-sized" and backed in white so that readers could simply cut them out and make their own "collectibles"—exactly like the imitation-antique bottles, jars, cans, and boxes that sell for rather high prices in gift shops.

Once cut out, these labels can be pasted down directly onto an ordinary metal can, using any commercial glue or clear tape. The larger ones, often from boxes, can be framed to produce delightful and decorative pictures; the smaller ones, usually from bottles, can be pasted onto any clear bottle or jar purchased in a five-and-ten-cent store. These are just a few ideas, but use your imagination! A museum we know created an entire "country store" by making color photocopies of some of our labels and pasting them onto cans. The room looked fabulous—and you can do the same with ease and economy.

We hope you will enjoy these labels almost as much as we have enjoyed not only collecting them but also putting them together in this book for you. Have fun!

Ralph Kovel

Terry Kovel

October 1981

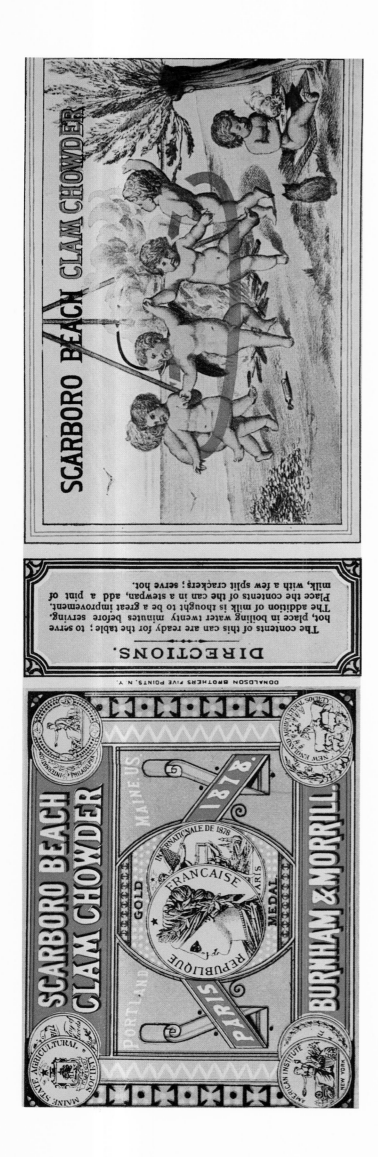

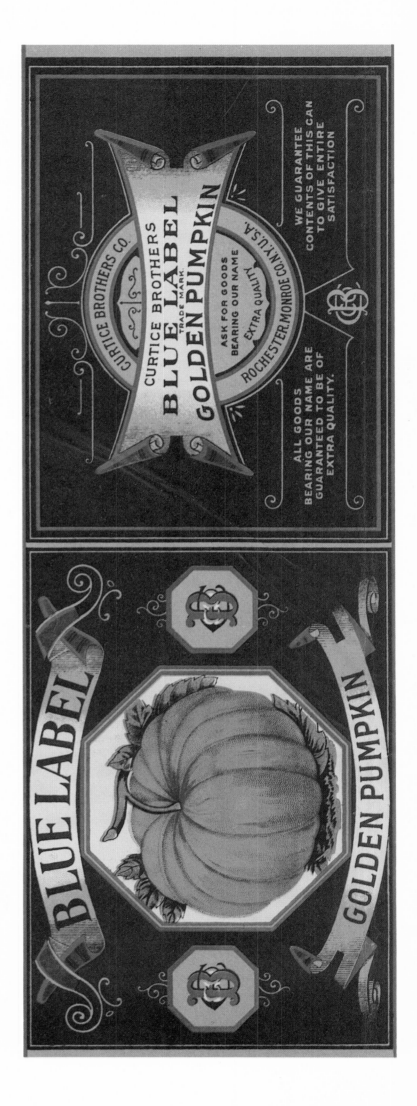

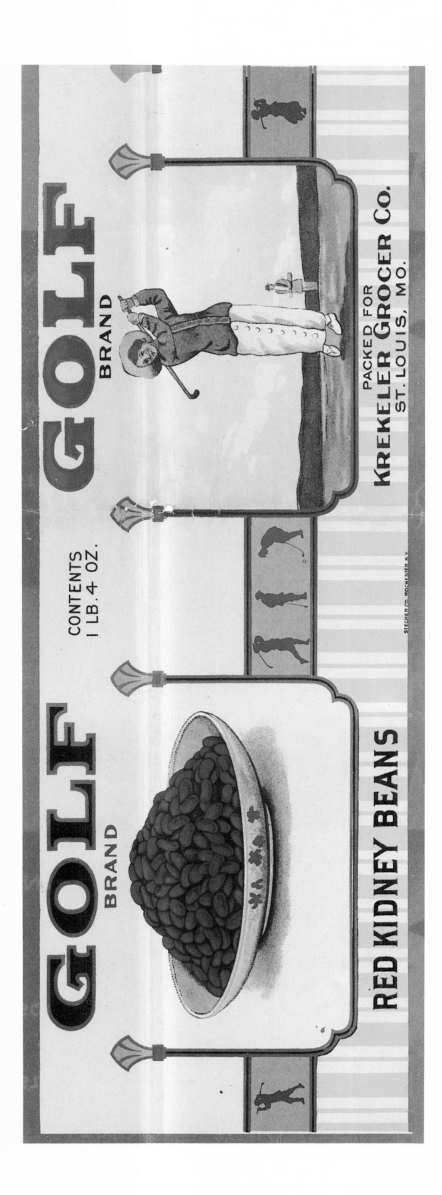

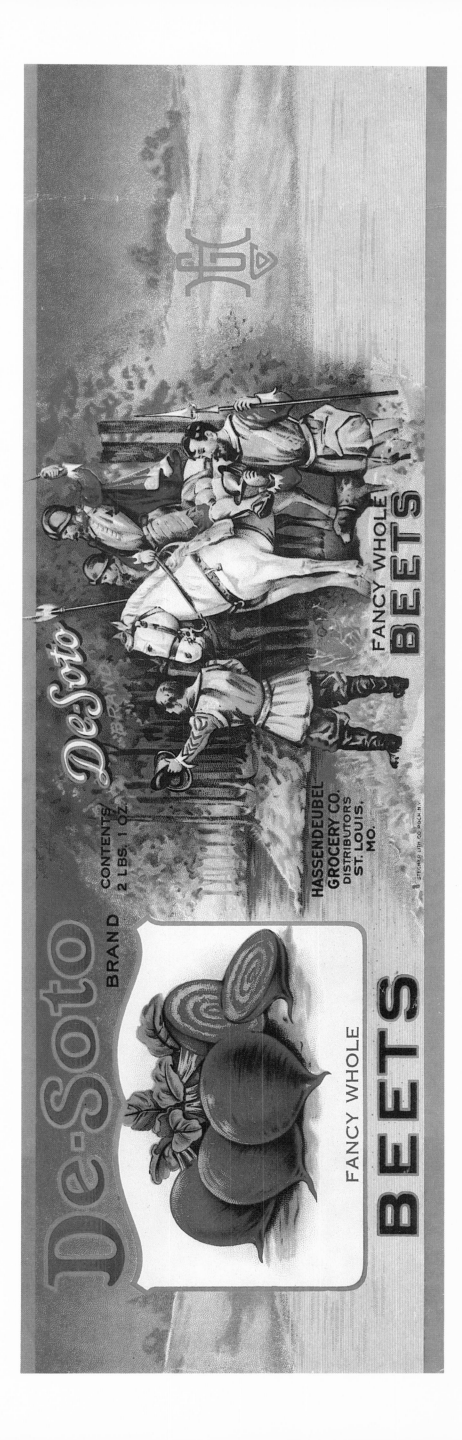

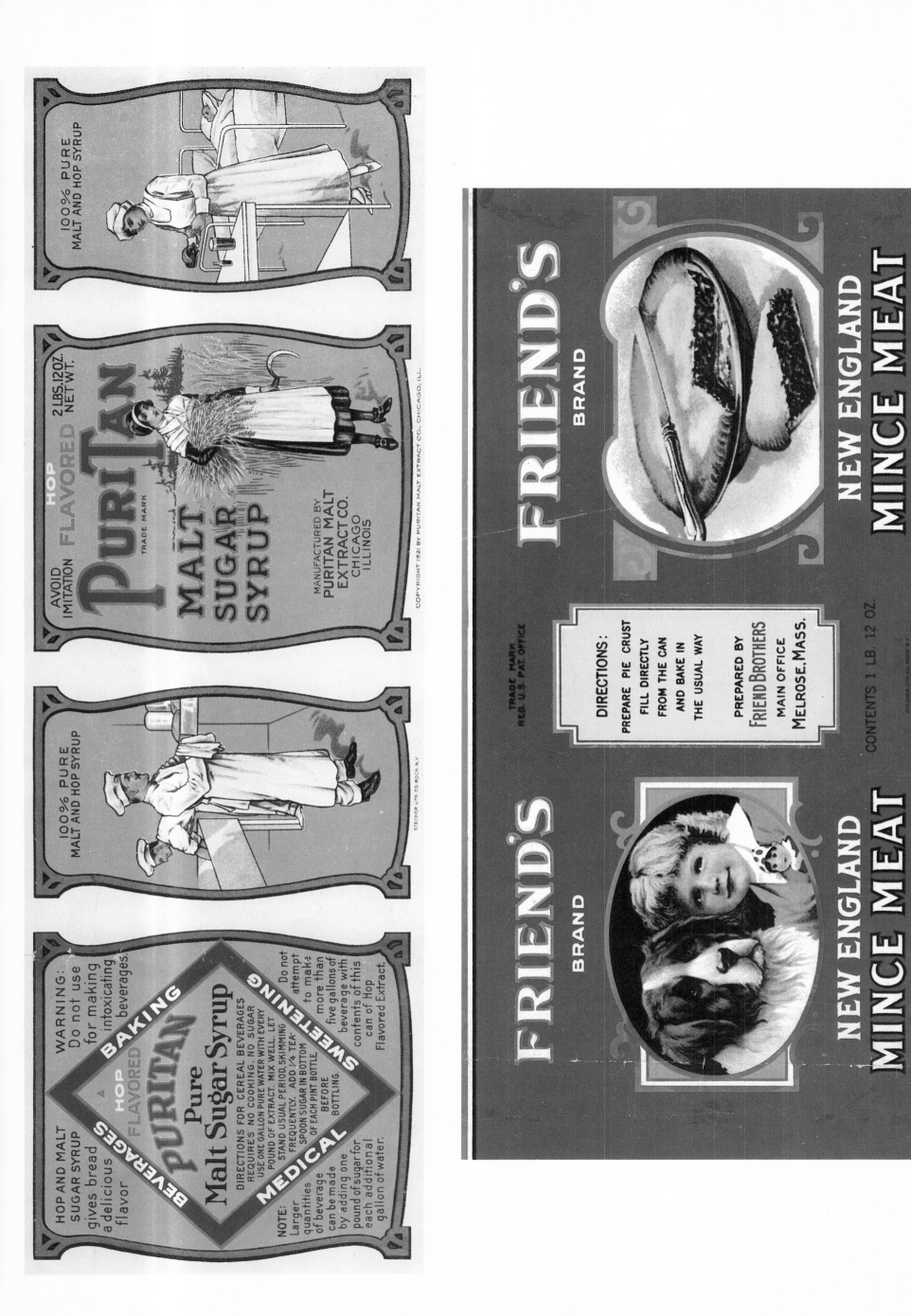

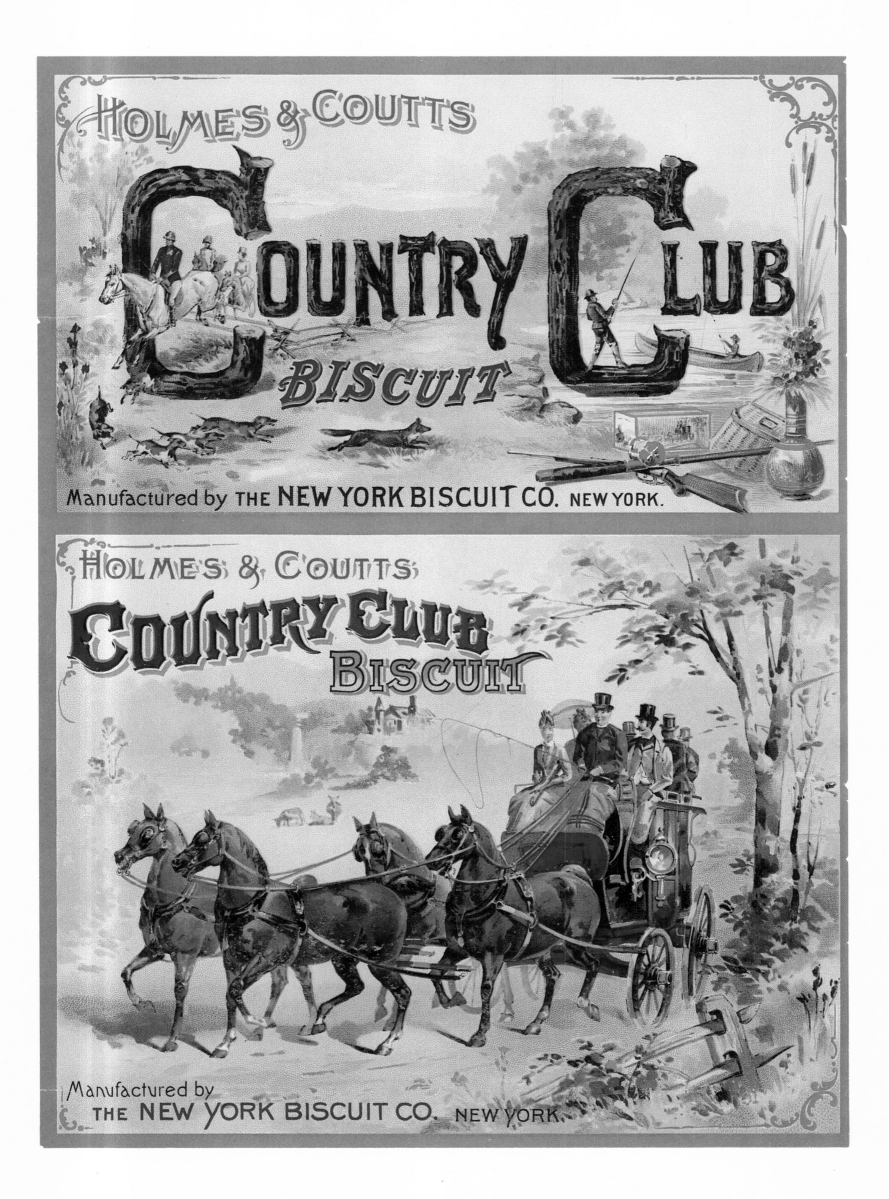

BOTTLED UNDER AUTHORITY OF THE
Coca-Cola
REG. U.S. PAT. OFF.
COPYRIGHT 1907, BY COCA-COLA CO.
COCA-COLA CO. ATLANTA, GA.
MINIMUM VOLUME 6½ OZ.

MORNING SIP
DRY
ROAST COFFEE
ALEX. SHEPPARD & SONS.
INC.
PHILADELPHIA.
COPYRIGHTED

A SPARKLING
BEVERAGE
Pepsi-Cola
TRADE MARK
REG. U.S. PAT. OFF.
CONTENTS 12 FL. OZ.
REFRESHING-SATISFYING